PRINCEWILL LAGANG

The Oracle of Silicon Valley: Larry Ellison's Trailblazing Journey in Tech Dominance

First published by PRINCEWILL LAGANG 2023

Copyright © 2023 by Princewill Lagang

All rights reserved. No part of this publication may be reproduced, stored or transmitted in any form or by any means, electronic, mechanical, photocopying, recording, scanning, or otherwise without written permission from the publisher. It is illegal to copy this book, post it to a website, or distribute it by any other means without permission.

Princewill Lagang asserts the moral right to be identified as the author of this work.

First edition

This book was professionally typeset on Reedsy.
Find out more at reedsy.com

Contents

1. Genesis of a Visionary — 1
2. The Rise of Oracle — 4
3. The Global Tech Titan — 7
4. Legacy in Motion — 10
5. The Oracle's Enduring Flame — 13
6. A Timeless Oracle — 16
7. A Tapestry Unfinished — 19
8. Beyond the Horizon — 22
9. The Tapestry Unfolds — 25
10. Horizons of Possibility — 28
11. Eclipses and Dawns — 31
12. The Ever-Flowing Stream — 34
13. Summary — 37

Contents

1	Genesis of a Visionary	1
2	The Rise of Oracle	4
3	The Global Tech Titan	7
4	Legacy in Motion	10
5	The Oracle's Enduring Flame	13
6	A Timeless Oracle	16
7	A Tapestry Unfinished	19
8	Beyond the Horizon	22
9	The Tapestry Unfolds	25
10	Horizons of Possibility	28
11	Eclipses and Dawns	31
12	The Ever-Flowing Stream	34
13	Summary	37

1

Genesis of a Visionary

In the heart of the Silicon Valley, where innovation thrives and dreams take flight, a technological titan emerged from the shadows, poised to shape the future of the digital landscape. This is the story of Larry Ellison, the Oracle of Silicon Valley, and the trailblazing journey that catapulted him into the realm of tech dominance.

The Birth of a Visionary

The year was 1944, and Larry Ellison entered the world in the bustling city of New York. From the outset, Ellison displayed an insatiable curiosity and an irrepressible drive, foreshadowing the brilliance that would later define his career. As a young boy, he exhibited an affinity for mathematics and an uncanny ability to dissect complex problems—a talent that would become the cornerstone of his future success.

The Turbulent Tide of Early Adversity

Ellison's childhood was not without its challenges. Raised by his aunt and uncle, he faced financial struggles and societal adversity. Yet, in the face of these obstacles, Ellison's resilience and determination forged a path forward. His early experiences instilled in him a relentless pursuit of success and a refusal to accept mediocrity.

The Spark of Innovation

Ellison's journey into the tech realm commenced during his time at the University of Illinois, where he discovered a passion for computer science. The era was marked by the burgeoning possibilities of computing, and Ellison, ever the visionary, foresaw the transformative power of technology. This realization sparked a fervor within him—an unyielding desire to harness the potential of computing for unprecedented feats.

Silicon Valley Beckons

In the early 1970s, Ellison migrated westward, drawn to the epicenter of technological innovation—Silicon Valley. Here, amid the palm-lined streets and nondescript office parks, he envisioned a future where computers would not only process data but also intuitively understand and respond to human queries. This audacious vision laid the foundation for what would become Oracle Corporation.

The Genesis of Oracle Corporation

Chapter 1 delves into the pivotal moments that led to the birth of Oracle Corporation. Ellison, alongside his co-founders, Bob Miner and Ed Oates, embarked on a mission to create a relational database management system—a groundbreaking concept at the time. Their collaboration marked the genesis of Oracle, a name chosen to evoke the prophetic qualities of a database that could foretell the future of data management.

A Glimpse into Chapter 2

As we close the inaugural chapter of Larry Ellison's journey, the stage is set for the ascension of Oracle Corporation. Chapter 2 will explore the trials and triumphs as Ellison navigates the dynamic landscape of Silicon Valley, shaping Oracle into a technological juggernaut and himself into an enigmatic figure synonymous with innovation and dominance. Join us on this captivating odyssey through the life and legacy of the Oracle of Silicon Valley.

2

The Rise of Oracle

The Silicon Crucible

As Larry Ellison and his co-founders, Bob Miner and Ed Oates, set out to establish Oracle Corporation, Silicon Valley was undergoing a transformative period. The air was charged with the excitement of possibility, and the trio, undeterred by the skeptics, dove headfirst into the crucible of innovation. Oracle's mission was ambitious: to develop a relational database management system capable of handling vast amounts of data with unprecedented efficiency.

The Battle for Relevance

The early days were fraught with challenges. Oracle faced competition from established players and skepticism regarding the feasibility of relational databases. Ellison, however, armed with his unwavering conviction, spearheaded the company through the tumultuous terrain. The team at Oracle relentlessly refined their product, anticipating the needs of an evolving digital landscape.

The Breakthrough: Oracle Database

Chapter 2 delves into the watershed moment when Oracle Database emerged as a technological marvel. With its revolutionary architecture, the database not only organized data but also allowed for complex queries, setting a new standard in the industry. Businesses began to take notice of Oracle's capabilities, marking the beginning of a trajectory that would see the company rise to prominence.

Expanding Horizons

Ellison's visionary leadership propelled Oracle beyond the database realm. Recognizing the potential for comprehensive solutions, the company broadened its offerings. Chapter 2 explores Oracle's foray into applications, middleware, and other technologies, showcasing Ellison's ability to anticipate the market's demands and stay one step ahead.

Mergers and Acquisitions

As Oracle grew, so did its appetite for expansion. Chapter 2 unravels the strategic mergers and acquisitions orchestrated by Ellison, each move calculated to fortify Oracle's position in the tech ecosystem. The company's portfolio expanded, encompassing diverse technologies and industries, solidifying Oracle's status as a multifaceted powerhouse.

The Enigma of Larry Ellison

Beyond the boardrooms and product launches, Chapter 2 delves into the enigmatic personality of Larry Ellison. An unconventional leader with a penchant for sailing and a taste for adventure, Ellison became a symbol of Silicon Valley's bold spirit. His public persona and management style added layers to the narrative, painting a portrait of a leader who was as unpredictable as he was visionary.

Teaser for Chapter 3

As we conclude Chapter 2, Oracle stands at the precipice of a new era. The stage is set for Oracle to not only dominate the tech landscape but also redefine the rules of the game. Chapter 3 will unveil the challenges and triumphs as Oracle cements its position as a global tech giant, and Larry Ellison's influence extends far beyond the borders of Silicon Valley. Join us on this riveting journey through the Oracle of Silicon Valley's ascent to tech supremacy.

3

The Global Tech Titan

Oracle's Global Ascent

The dawn of the 21st century saw Oracle Corporation evolve into a global tech titan under Larry Ellison's unwavering guidance. Chapter 3 explores the pivotal moments that propelled Oracle beyond Silicon Valley, transforming it into a force to be reckoned with on the international stage. The company's products and services became integral to businesses worldwide, cementing its status as a linchpin of the digital era.

Cloud Computing Revolution

As the technological landscape continued to shift, Ellison foresaw the rise of cloud computing as the next frontier. Chapter 3 delves into Oracle's strategic pivot towards cloud services, a move that would redefine the company's role in the industry. Ellison's vision for a comprehensive cloud platform, encompassing infrastructure, applications, and platform services, set Oracle on a trajectory to dominate the cloud computing space.

Challenges and Adaptations

No ascent to dominance is without its challenges. Chapter 3 uncovers the obstacles Oracle faced in an ever-evolving tech landscape. The dot-com bubble, economic downturns, and technological disruptions tested Oracle's resilience. Ellison's adaptive leadership style and strategic maneuvers allowed the company not only to weather these storms but also to emerge stronger and more innovative.

The Autonomous Database

A highlight of this chapter is Oracle's groundbreaking Autonomous Database. Ellison's vision for a self-driving, self-securing, and self-repairing database revolutionized data management. Chapter 3 delves into the development of this cutting-edge technology and its impact on Oracle's standing in the market.

Beyond Databases: Oracle's Diversification

Oracle's dominance extended beyond databases and cloud services. Chapter 3 explores the company's diversification into emerging technologies such as artificial intelligence, machine learning, and blockchain. Ellison's commitment to staying at the forefront of innovation positioned Oracle as a leader in shaping the technological landscape of the future.

The Philanthropic Oracle

Chapter 3 also sheds light on Larry Ellison's philanthropic endeavors. As Oracle's success soared, Ellison turned his attention to using his wealth for the greater good. The chapter explores his contributions to education, healthcare, and environmental causes, showcasing a multifaceted leader who recognized the responsibility that comes with influence.

The Legacy Unfolds

As we wrap up Chapter 3, Oracle Corporation stands as a testament to Larry Ellison's visionary leadership. The company's global influence, technological innovations, and philanthropic efforts have left an indelible mark on the world. Chapter 4 will delve into the latter years of Ellison's career, examining his impact on the tech industry's future and the enduring legacy he crafted as the Oracle of Silicon Valley. Join us on the final leg of this compelling journey through Larry Ellison's trailblazing career.

4

Legacy in Motion

The Later Years of Larry Ellison

As Larry Ellison traversed the later years of his illustrious career, Chapter 4 peels back the layers of the man behind the Oracle of Silicon Valley. Ellison's leadership style, business acumen, and continued pursuit of technological innovation continued to shape Oracle and the broader tech landscape.

Oracle's Continued Technological Dominance

Despite the ever-changing nature of the tech industry, Oracle, under Ellison's guidance, remained a stalwart presence. Chapter 4 delves into Oracle's ongoing commitment to technological excellence and its role in shaping the digital future. The company's advancements in artificial intelligence, cloud computing, and data management solidified its standing as an industry leader.

Shaping the Cloud Landscape

Ellison's vision for Oracle Cloud continued to unfold. Chapter 4 explores the company's strides in cloud infrastructure, platform, and application services. The Autonomous Database, pioneered in the previous chapter, evolved and matured, setting new standards for efficiency, security, and reliability in the cloud.

Leadership in a Time of Change

With the tech industry undergoing rapid transformations, Ellison's leadership took center stage in Chapter 4. His strategic decisions and ability to navigate Oracle through economic uncertainties and disruptive innovations showcased a leader unafraid to embrace change. The chapter examines how Ellison's adaptability played a pivotal role in Oracle's continued success.

Cultural Impact and Innovation

Beyond business strategy, Chapter 4 delves into the cultural impact of Oracle and Ellison's influence on fostering innovation within the organization. The company's commitment to diversity, employee development, and a culture of continuous improvement contributed to Oracle's legacy as more than just a tech giant but a hub of creativity and forward-thinking.

Ellison's Enduring Vision

As Ellison approached the twilight of his career, Chapter 4 explores how his original vision for Oracle manifested on a global scale. The company's products and services became integral not only to businesses but also to governments, educational institutions, and various industries, leaving an indelible mark on the world's digital infrastructure.

The Philanthropic Continuum

Chapter 4 sheds light on Larry Ellison's philanthropic efforts in the later years.

The Ellison Medical Foundation, environmental initiatives, and educational contributions underscored his commitment to giving back. The Oracle of Silicon Valley's impact extended beyond technology into realms that touched the lives of people around the globe.

The Final Chapter Beckons

As we conclude Chapter 4, Larry Ellison's legacy is in full view. The final chapter awaits, providing a retrospective on the Oracle of Silicon Valley's enduring impact on the tech industry, the global community, and the future of innovation. Join us for the culmination of this captivating journey through the life and legacy of Larry Ellison.

5

The Oracle's Enduring Flame

A Retrospective on Innovation

In the closing chapter of this narrative, we reflect on the enduring legacy of Larry Ellison and Oracle Corporation. Chapter 5 serves as a retrospective on the innovations, challenges, and transformative moments that defined Ellison's journey and Oracle's ascent to tech supremacy.

Technological Landscape in Transition

As Chapter 5 unfolds, we explore how Oracle adapted to the ever-changing technological landscape. The emergence of new paradigms, from the Internet of Things to quantum computing, presented both challenges and opportunities. Ellison's foresight and Oracle's continued commitment to innovation positioned the company as a guiding force in navigating the complexities of a rapidly evolving digital era.

A Lasting Impact on Industry Dynamics

Delving into the latter years, we examine Ellison's influence on industry dynamics. Oracle's strategic partnerships, collaborations, and contributions to open-source communities come to the forefront. Chapter 5 illuminates how Oracle's interactions with competitors and collaborators shaped not only the company's trajectory but also the broader tech ecosystem.

Leadership Transition and Oracle's Future

With Larry Ellison's eventual retirement, Chapter 5 explores the transition of leadership within Oracle. The narrative unfolds as new leaders step into Ellison's formidable shoes, tasked with sustaining and building upon the legacy of innovation and dominance. The chapter provides insights into Oracle's strategic roadmap and its role in shaping the future of technology.

The Human Side of Larry Ellison

In this concluding chapter, we delve into the personal side of Larry Ellison. Beyond the boardrooms and product launches, Ellison's personality, passions, and pursuits outside the tech realm come into focus. Chapter 5 offers a nuanced perspective on the man behind the Oracle, exploring the intersection of his personal and professional life.

Oracle's Ongoing Philanthropy

Chapter 5 sheds light on Oracle's continued commitment to philanthropy. As the company solidified its place as a global tech giant, its contributions to societal causes intensified. The chapter highlights Oracle's philanthropic initiatives and how the company, even beyond Ellison's direct involvement, remained dedicated to making a positive impact on the world.

The Oracle Legacy: Looking Forward

As we draw the curtain on this narrative, Chapter 5 peers into the future. The enduring flame of the Oracle legacy continues to illuminate the path for the next generation of tech leaders. The chapter concludes with a reflection on how Larry Ellison's journey and Oracle Corporation's legacy will inspire, shape, and influence the unfolding chapters of technological innovation.

Epilogue: A Timeless Oracle

In the epilogue, we cast a gaze into the timelessness of the Oracle's legacy. Larry Ellison's trailblazing journey in tech dominance, the evolution of Oracle Corporation, and the impact on the tech industry transcend the boundaries of time. The Oracle's flame, kindled in Silicon Valley, continues to burn brightly, illuminating the way for those who dare to dream, innovate, and shape the future.

6

A Timeless Oracle

The Enduring Echo of Innovation

In this concluding chapter, we step back to witness the timeless reverberations of Larry Ellison's trailblazing journey and Oracle Corporation's legacy. Chapter 6 serves as an epilogue, capturing the enduring echo of innovation, influence, and impact that transcends the temporal confines of Silicon Valley.

The Ripple Effect

As the story of Larry Ellison and Oracle Corporation comes to a close, Chapter 6 explores the ripple effect of their contributions to the tech industry. The innovations, technologies, and business strategies set in motion continue to influence and shape the way societies across the globe interact with information, data, and each other.

Oracle's Continued Evolution

While Larry Ellison's direct involvement in Oracle may have evolved, Chapter

6 investigates how the company continued to evolve. New leadership, fresh perspectives, and ongoing commitments to innovation ensure that Oracle remains a dynamic force in the tech landscape, adapting to emerging trends and pushing the boundaries of what is possible.

The Tech Landscape of Tomorrow

Delving into the future, this chapter casts a speculative eye on the tech landscape of tomorrow. How will Oracle's legacy influence the next wave of technological advancements? What role will the company play in shaping the digital frontiers of artificial intelligence, quantum computing, and beyond? Chapter 6 invites readers to contemplate the potential trajectories of Oracle and the broader tech industry.

Lessons from the Oracle

As the epilogue unfolds, it distills the lessons embedded in Larry Ellison's journey. From the importance of visionary leadership to the resilience needed to navigate a volatile industry, Chapter 6 encapsulates the wisdom garnered from the Oracle's experiences. These lessons stand as beacons for aspiring entrepreneurs, technologists, and leaders charting their own courses in the world of innovation.

The Oracle Legacy: Beyond Tech

Chapter 6 takes a holistic view of the Oracle legacy, extending beyond the realm of technology. The philanthropic endeavors initiated by Larry Ellison and Oracle Corporation continue to leave a positive impact on education, healthcare, and environmental sustainability. The chapter contemplates how these contributions contribute to a legacy of social responsibility and corporate citizenship.

A Call to the Future

The concluding chapter is not merely an endpoint but a call to the future. As we bid farewell to the narrative of Larry Ellison and Oracle Corporation, it prompts readers to consider their roles in the ongoing narrative of innovation. How will today's leaders and visionaries contribute to the ever-evolving story of technology?

Legacy in Perpetuity

In the final pages, Chapter 6 leaves readers with a sense of awe and inspiration, underscoring that the legacy of Larry Ellison and Oracle Corporation is not confined to a specific era or chapter. It is a legacy in perpetuity—an eternal flame that continues to light the way for those who dare to dream, create, and shape the future.

7

A Tapestry Unfinished

As we turn the page to Chapter 7, we find ourselves in a narrative space that extends beyond the confines of the preceding chapters. Here, we explore the unfolding tapestry of the tech industry and Oracle Corporation, recognizing that the story is ongoing, dynamic, and shaped by the interplay of countless threads—innovations, challenges, and the visionaries who continue to propel the industry forward.

The Evolving Landscape

Chapter 7 opens with a panoramic view of the ever-evolving tech landscape. From artificial intelligence to biotechnology, the technological tapestry is woven with threads of innovation that stretch far beyond the conventional boundaries. The narrative captures the spirit of continual change, setting the stage for a discussion on how Oracle and its counterparts navigate this uncharted territory.

Oracle's Next Chapter

Diving into Oracle's trajectory, Chapter 7 examines the company's ongoing journey. With new leadership at the helm and a commitment to staying at the forefront of technological advancements, Oracle's narrative continues to unfold. The chapter explores the company's strategies, partnerships, and innovations that position it as a key player in shaping the digital future.

Challenges and Triumphs

The narrative doesn't shy away from the challenges that lie ahead. Chapter 7 delves into the hurdles faced by Oracle and the broader tech industry—cybersecurity threats, ethical considerations in AI development, and the ever-present need for agility in the face of rapidly changing market dynamics. However, it also celebrates the triumphs and breakthroughs that define this chapter of technological evolution.

The Visionaries of Tomorrow

As we progress, Chapter 7 introduces the visionaries and disruptors who are shaping the next era of technology. The narrative shines a spotlight on emerging leaders, startups, and bold initiatives that are pushing the boundaries of what is conceivable. It asks the question: who are the Larry Ellisons of tomorrow, and what stories will they inscribe on the digital canvas?

Beyond Silicon Valley

The scope broadens as Chapter 7 explores the global nature of technological innovation. The narrative unfolds in regions beyond Silicon Valley, recognizing the diverse landscapes where tech ecosystems are flourishing. From burgeoning tech hubs in Asia to innovation clusters in Europe, the chapter paints a picture of a global tapestry woven with threads of creativity and progress.

Societal Impact and Responsibility

Beyond technology itself, the narrative in Chapter 7 contemplates the societal impact of the tech industry. Themes of ethical responsibility, sustainability, and inclusivity come to the forefront. It reflects on how companies like Oracle navigate the complex interplay between innovation and the broader social and environmental context.

The Unfinished Tapestry

As Chapter 7 draws to a close, it leaves readers with a sense of anticipation—a recognition that the tapestry being woven is far from complete. The narrative arc extends into the horizon, and the stories of Larry Ellison, Oracle Corporation, and the broader tech industry continue to unfold, intertwining with the aspirations, challenges, and innovations of generations to come.

An Invitation to the Reader

The concluding chapter extends an invitation to the reader to participate in shaping the narrative. It challenges individuals to contribute to the ongoing story of technology, innovation, and progress. As we close the book on this chapter, we recognize that the tapestry remains unfinished, and the pages of the future are waiting to be written by those bold enough to dream, create, and lead.

8

Beyond the Horizon

As we embark on the final chapter of this narrative, we step into a realm that extends beyond the immediate confines of the tech industry, beyond the chronicles of Oracle and the Silicon Valley pioneers. Chapter 8 is an exploration of the limitless possibilities, the uncharted territories, and the collective endeavors that shape the ever-expanding horizon of human progress.

The Interconnected Future

Chapter 8 opens with a contemplation of the interconnected nature of our world. The narrative weaves together threads of technology, society, and the environment, emphasizing the symbiotic relationship that defines the future. From smart cities to global collaborations, the story unfolds as a tapestry of interconnected innovations.

Emergent Technologies

Diving into the heart of innovation, the chapter examines emergent technologies that have the potential to redefine the human experience. From the intricacies of quantum computing to the possibilities offered by biotechnology and space exploration, Chapter 8 paints a picture of a future shaped by the convergence of diverse technological frontiers.

Inclusive and Ethical Tech

The narrative takes a turn toward the ethical considerations of our technological future. Chapter 8 reflects on the importance of inclusivity, ethical development, and responsible deployment of technology. It explores how the tech industry can be a force for positive change, addressing societal challenges and fostering a more equitable world.

Collaborative Ventures

The story extends beyond individual companies as Chapter 8 delves into the power of collaborative ventures. Partnerships between industry leaders, startups, and cross-sector collaborations become instrumental in addressing global challenges. The narrative highlights the potential of collective efforts in driving innovation and creating meaningful impact.

Shaping the Future Workforce

Anticipating the needs of a rapidly evolving landscape, the chapter explores the future of work and the skills that will be crucial for the workforce of tomorrow. The narrative considers how education, training, and adaptability will play pivotal roles in preparing individuals for the challenges and opportunities that lie ahead.

Sustainability Imperative

With a keen focus on the environmental landscape, Chapter 8 underscores the imperative of sustainability. The narrative explores how technology can be harnessed to address climate change, promote sustainable practices, and contribute to a harmonious coexistence with the planet.

The Human Element

Amidst the technological tapestry, Chapter 8 reintroduces the human element. The narrative contemplates the role of human creativity, empathy, and resilience in shaping the future. It emphasizes that, while technology is a powerful tool, the values and intentions of those wielding it are pivotal in determining its impact.

An Ongoing Narrative

As Chapter 8 draws to a close, it leaves the reader with a sense of continuity. The narrative is not an endpoint but a waypoint—a moment in an ongoing journey. The horizon, ever-expanding, invites individuals, organizations, and societies to contribute their chapters to the collective story of human progress.

A Call to Action

The concluding chapter extends a call to action—a call for active participation in shaping the future. It challenges the reader to be architects of positive change, stewards of innovation, and champions of a future that reflects the best of our collective aspirations.

The Uncharted Tomorrow

In the final pages, Chapter 8 fades into the uncharted expanse of tomorrow. The narrative echoes the sentiment that, beyond the pages of this story, beyond the known and familiar, lies a vast landscape of possibilities waiting to be explored, shaped, and embraced by those who dare to imagine and pioneer.

9

The Tapestry Unfolds

As we enter Chapter 9, the narrative takes a reflective turn, focusing on the unfolding tapestry of the collective human journey into the future. This chapter encapsulates the dynamic interplay of innovation, resilience, and the relentless pursuit of progress that characterizes the evolving narrative of our shared existence.

Threads of Continuity

Chapter 9 opens with an exploration of the threads of continuity that weave through the fabric of human history. It reflects on the lessons learned, the wisdom gained, and the enduring qualities of the human spirit that persist across generations. The narrative invites readers to consider the rich tapestry of human achievement and the potential for future threads to be woven into this intricate design.

Cultural Perspectives on Innovation

Diving into the diverse cultural perspectives that shape the global narrative, the chapter highlights the richness of human creativity. It explores how different societies contribute unique threads to the tapestry of innovation, emphasizing the importance of cultural diversity in fostering a truly global exchange of ideas.

Navigating Uncertainty

As the narrative unfolds, Chapter 9 addresses the inevitability of uncertainty on the path forward. It acknowledges the unpredictable nature of the future and explores strategies for navigating ambiguity, embracing change, and cultivating resilience in the face of unforeseen challenges.

Intertwining Narratives

The chapter weaves together the intertwining narratives of individuals, communities, and nations. It examines the interconnectedness of our stories and the potential for collaborative efforts to shape a future that transcends borders, fostering a sense of shared responsibility for the well-being of the planet and its inhabitants.

The Tapestry of Wisdom

Reflecting on the collective wisdom garnered through centuries of human experience, Chapter 9 contemplates the importance of passing down knowledge to future generations. It explores how the tapestry of wisdom, woven with threads of innovation and tradition, becomes a guide for navigating the complexities of an ever-evolving world.

Transformative Technologies

The narrative shifts focus to transformative technologies that have the potential to reshape the very fabric of human existence. From advancements in medicine and artificial intelligence to breakthroughs in sustainable energy, Chapter 9 envisions how these technologies might contribute to a narrative of positive change and human betterment.

Ethical Imperatives

Building upon the ethical considerations introduced in earlier chapters, this section delves deeper into the moral imperatives that accompany technological progress. It explores how societies can collectively establish ethical frameworks, ensuring that innovation aligns with values of justice, equality, and human dignity.

The Unwritten Chapters

As Chapter 9 approaches its conclusion, it leaves space for the unwritten chapters of the future. The narrative underscores the agency of individuals and communities to contribute their unique threads to the unfolding tapestry, inviting readers to consider their roles as authors of the next chapters in the story of human progress.

A Vision for Tomorrow

In the final pages, Chapter 9 offers a vision for tomorrow—a vision shaped by the collective efforts of individuals committed to the principles of innovation, sustainability, and human flourishing. It leaves the reader with a sense of anticipation, as the tapestry of the future continues to unfold, propelled by the aspirations and actions of those who dare to dream and create.

10

Horizons of Possibility

In this culminating chapter, we cast our gaze towards the horizons of possibility, embracing the boundless potential that lies ahead. Chapter 10 serves as both a reflection on the journey thus far and a bold exploration of the limitless frontiers awaiting the human narrative.

Reflecting on the Odyssey

As we embark on the final chapter, there is a moment of reflection on the odyssey woven throughout the narrative. Chapter 10 revisits key milestones, transformative moments, and the overarching themes that have shaped the story, inviting readers to consider the cumulative impact of the journey.

The Uncharted Frontier

The narrative pivots to the uncharted frontier, contemplating the territories yet to be explored. Chapter 10 sparks curiosity about the unknown, encouraging a spirit of discovery and innovation. It recognizes that the human narrative is an ever-evolving expedition into realms where possibilities are limited only by our collective imagination.

Transcending Boundaries

Chapter 10 explores the concept of transcending boundaries—geographical, technological, and societal. It delves into how breakthroughs in communication, collaboration, and understanding can foster a global community united by a shared vision for a better, more interconnected world.

Synergy of Disciplines

A central theme of the chapter is the synergy of disciplines. It celebrates the convergence of diverse fields—science, arts, technology, and humanities—and how the interplay between these disciplines sparks new ideas, innovations, and solutions that propel humanity forward.

Human Potential Unleashed

In contemplating the horizons, Chapter 10 envisions the unleashing of human potential. It explores how education, technology, and a commitment to lifelong learning can empower individuals to contribute meaningfully to the narrative of progress, fostering a society where each person is an active agent of positive change.

Empathy and Collective Well-being

At the heart of the narrative lies a focus on empathy and collective well-being. Chapter 10 explores how a deepened understanding of one another's experiences can foster a more compassionate and harmonious world, where the well-being of individuals and communities is intricately woven into the fabric of societal progress.

Environmental Stewardship

Environmental stewardship takes center stage as the narrative acknowledges the pressing need for sustainable practices. Chapter 10 contemplates how the collective effort to protect and regenerate the environment is integral to ensuring a vibrant and flourishing future for generations to come.

Redefining Success

The chapter invites a reevaluation of success. Beyond traditional metrics, it explores a broader definition—one that encompasses not only individual achievements but also contributions to the common good, the preservation of the planet, and the nurturing of a more equitable and inclusive global society.

A Call to Action

As Chapter 10 draws to a close, it issues a resounding call to action. It challenges readers to be architects of the future, active participants in shaping the unfolding narrative, and stewards of a world where possibilities are not limited by circumstance but propelled by collective vision and purpose.

A Timeless Tapestry

In the final passages, Chapter 10 fades into the distance, leaving the reader with a sense of optimism and responsibility. The tapestry of human progress, while shaped by the past, extends into the future—an ever-evolving narrative awaiting the creative input and courageous endeavors of those who dare to chart new courses and explore the vast horizons of possibility.

11

Eclipses and Dawns

As we venture into Chapter 11, the narrative takes on an introspective tone, exploring the cyclical nature of progress, the inevitable eclipses, and the resplendent dawns that follow. This chapter serves as a contemplative space, acknowledging that within every shadow, there is the potential for illumination.

Cycles of Innovation

Chapter 11 opens by acknowledging the cycles inherent in the journey of innovation. It reflects on historical patterns where periods of groundbreaking advancement are followed by moments of recalibration and reassessment. This introspection prompts readers to consider the rhythmic nature of progress.

The Eclipse of Challenges

As the narrative delves into the shadows, Chapter 11 unveils the eclipses—those challenging moments that cast temporary shadows on the landscape of progress. These challenges, whether technological, societal, or environmental, are examined not as insurmountable obstacles but as opportunities for resilience and growth.

Lessons from Darkness

Within the darkness of challenges, the chapter extracts lessons—lessons about adaptability, perseverance, and the human capacity for innovation even in the face of adversity. It invites readers to reflect on their own experiences of overcoming setbacks and finding light within the shadows.

Illumination in Unlikely Places

Chapter 11 turns to the theme of unexpected illumination. It explores how moments of ingenuity often emerge from the most unexpected places, emphasizing the importance of embracing diverse perspectives and finding inspiration in the unlikeliest of circumstances.

Societal Eclipses

The narrative broadens its focus to societal eclipses—moments when collective challenges cast shadows on progress. Whether addressing systemic inequalities, geopolitical tensions, or ethical dilemmas, Chapter 11 prompts readers to consider how these societal eclipses can be opportunities for meaningful transformation.

The Dawn of Collaborative Solutions

As the narrative progresses, Chapter 11 introduces the dawn—the emergence of collaborative solutions. It explores how the coming together of minds, resources, and communities can illuminate the path forward, leading to innovations that address both local and global challenges.

Technological Renaissance

In the context of technological evolution, the chapter contemplates the potential for a renaissance—a period of renewed creativity, breakthroughs, and paradigm shifts. It encourages readers to envision a future where technology becomes a catalyst for positive change and societal betterment.

Ethical Enlightenment

Chapter 11 emphasizes the importance of ethical enlightenment—a collective awakening to the ethical dimensions of technological progress. It explores how societies can navigate the complexities of innovation with a heightened sense of responsibility, ensuring that progress aligns with values of justice, equity, and human dignity.

The Emergence of New Narratives

As the chapter draws to a close, it envisions the emergence of new narratives. These narratives transcend individual achievements and highlight collective stories of collaboration, resilience, and the continuous pursuit of a better future. It invites readers to contribute to the crafting of these narratives in their own lives and communities.

A Timeless Cycle

In the final passages, Chapter 11 fades into the timeless cycle of eclipses and dawns. It leaves readers with a sense of reflection and anticipation, recognizing that progress is an ongoing journey—a cycle of challenges and triumphs, shadows and illumination. The narrative of innovation, resilience, and human potential continues to unfold, offering infinite possibilities on the horizon.

12

The Ever-Flowing Stream

As we step into the final chapter of this narrative, Chapter 12 takes on a fluid and reflective quality, symbolizing the ever-flowing stream of human experience, knowledge, and progress. This concluding chapter encapsulates the essence of continuity, adaptation, and the perpetual pursuit of wisdom.

The Stream of Continuity

Chapter 12 opens with a contemplation of the stream of continuity—a symbolic representation of the unbroken flow of human endeavors across time. It reflects on the contributions of countless individuals and civilizations, emphasizing the interconnected nature of the human journey.

The Wisdom of the Flow

The narrative explores the wisdom embedded within the flow. Chapter 12 contemplates how each ripple in the stream, whether a moment of triumph or challenge, carries lessons and insights that contribute to the collective reservoir of human understanding. It invites readers to draw inspiration from the continuous current of wisdom.

The Adaptive Current

Focusing on adaptability, Chapter 12 acknowledges the dynamic nature of the stream. It explores how societies, cultures, and individuals adapt to the changing currents of technology, environment, and societal structures. This adaptability is seen as a source of resilience and innovation in the face of evolving challenges.

Navigating the Rapids of Change

As the narrative explores the metaphorical rapids of change, Chapter 12 delves into strategies for navigating these turbulent waters. It reflects on the importance of foresight, collaboration, and a shared commitment to ethical and sustainable practices as essential tools for steering through the complexities of progress.

Confluences of Innovation

The chapter introduces the concept of confluences—points where diverse streams of knowledge, cultures, and technologies converge. Chapter 12 explores how these confluences become fertile grounds for innovation, fostering the cross-pollination of ideas and the emergence of transformative solutions to global challenges.

The Ephemeral Beauty of Now

In contemplating the transient nature of time, the narrative reflects on the ephemeral beauty of the present moment. Chapter 12 encourages readers to savor the richness of the current era, recognizing that the choices made today contribute to the unfolding narrative of tomorrow.

The Legacy of Responsible Stewardship

A central theme emerges in the form of responsible stewardship. Chapter 12 explores how individuals and societies can act as stewards of the stream, safeguarding its health and ensuring that future generations inherit a world where the flow of progress is marked by ethical considerations and a commitment to collective well-being.

Echoes of Future Ripples

As the chapter nears its conclusion, it contemplates the echoes of future ripples. It encourages readers to consider the impact of their actions on the trajectory of the stream—how today's choices resonate through time, shaping the narrative for those who will follow.

An Invitation to the Riverbanks

In the final passages, Chapter 12 extends an invitation to the riverbanks. It symbolizes a space for reflection, collaboration, and shared contemplation. The narrative encourages readers to gather on the riverbanks of collective human experience, where the stream of progress flows ceaselessly, inviting all to contribute to the ever-expanding story of the human journey.

13

Summary

The narrative unfolds across twelve chapters, traversing the life and legacy of Larry Ellison, the evolution of Oracle Corporation, and ultimately expanding into broader reflections on the human journey and the future of innovation. From the trailblazing days in Silicon Valley to Oracle's global dominance, the story captures pivotal moments, challenges, and innovations. Each chapter explores themes such as adaptability, ethical considerations, and the societal impact of technology. The narrative concludes with contemplations on the uncharted territories of progress, acknowledging the cycles of challenges and triumphs, and inviting readers to be active participants in shaping a future where the stream of human progress flows responsibly, ethically, and with boundless possibilities.

www.ingramcontent.com/pod-product-compliance
Lightning Source LLC
LaVergne TN
LVHW021055100526
838202LV00083B/6002